Text Copyright © 2010 by Tim Caverly
Illustrations Copyright © 2010 by Franklin Manzo, Jr.
All Rights Reserved. Published by Tim Caverly

Library of Congress Cataloging-in-Publication Data
Caverly, Tim.
ALLAGASH TAILS: A collection of short stories from
Maine's Allagash Wilderness Waterway
Vol. III:
Wilderness Wildlife/Animal Antics From Our Nation's Premier
Wild and Scenic River
By Tim Caverly;
Illustrated by Franklin Manzo, Jr.
p. cm. - (Wildlife)
"Tim Caverly"
Summary: A Collection of "Tails" based on animal antics in
Maine's Northern wilderness.
ISBN 978-1-4507-3637-4
Printed in the U.S.A.
First Printing, November 2010

DEDICATION

For years there have been many people who have devoted themselves to protecting the Allagash. This book is dedicated to those who have spoken out for the wilderness experience that the Allagash River represents to our nation and the world.

ACKNOWLEDGEMENTS

"That's soooo cool," the young student softly muttered as she continued towards her next class. The teenager had stopped me in the hallway of our school to inquire if I was writing a new book for my "Allagash Tails" collection. I assured her that a Volume III, with new anecdotes from the Maine woods, "was in the works." As she walked away, her face lit up with a smile as she nodded to herself; *not only did she know an author, but he even worked in her school, sweeet!*

Even though I've always enjoyed putting words on paper to mold stories and compose random rhymes for my wife, daughter and friends (and one can find plenty of composition fodder in the Allagash river corridor) I've never considered myself an author. However, I do enjoy in sharing the experiences of my thirty-two years with the Maine Park Service.

This book was conceived because of the support and positive comments we had received from students about Volumes I and II. Their requests for more tales were so overwhelming that we thought it natural to ask pupils in Millinocket and far away Washington County to help with Volume III. I asked teachers for suggestions of students who they thought might like to contribute to this book through illustrating and editing. Those students were contacted and their response to our invitation was heartwarming.

We would like to thank student artists Travis

Hartley and Mike Debona from the Millinocket Middle School, and Joshua Perrotti from Stearns High School, for contributing illustrations.

We appreciate the editing that was done by students Alyssa Birmingham and Baleigh Studer of the Millinocket Middle School as well as Alayna Caricofe of the Edmunds Consolidated School and Preston Leighton of the Pembroke Elementary School.

All of the students were very dedicated to their work. One pupil told me that she was so worried about doing her best that, "I must have read my assigned story at least fifty times."

I specifically wish to thank Mary Miller of Oakfield for her contributions. All of their efforts have made this a more descriptive book about northern Maine's national treasure.

Tim Caverly

Millinocket, Maine

October 2010

FORWARD

As with our last book *An Allagash Haunting (Allagash Tails Volume II)*, this publication contains challenge words in bold print, supported by a glossary located in the back of the book.

While we wish to encourage students to read, it is also our desire to kindle a desire in people of all ages to learn about our state's spectacular natural area called the Allagash.

Our work has already begun on Allagash Tails Volume IV, *A Wilderness Rangers' Journal, Rendezvous at Devil's Elbow.* This book will be a sequel to the popular *An Allagash Haunting-The Story of Emile Camile,* and is scheduled for release in 2011.

In the tale *A Wilderness Rangers' Journal* the daughter of a former Allagash supervisor discovers her father's diary. Through her dad's forgotten words she will learn of daily adventures and personal challenges that their family experienced while living in the remote Maine woods.

For more information about *A Wilderness Rangers' Journal* please check our website at www.allagashtails. com

To read more of our Allagash adventures please ask your local bookstore for copies of our other books *Allagash Tails Volume I* and *Allagash Tails Volume II- "An Allagash Haunting-The Story of Emile Camile.*

INTRODUCTION

My partner, Franklin Manzo Jr. and I are pleased to present Volume III of our *Allagash Tails* collection of short stories . Once again, as in Volumes I and II, these anecdotes come directly from the Allagash River, deep in the remote North Maine Woods.

Talk with anyone who has traveled this spectacular National Wild and Scenic River and they will eagerly share a treasure trove of experiences. I am happy to share my adventures as well. These tales sprouted from personal adventures that I had during my eighteen years as Supervisor of the 140,000-acre river corridor for Maine's Department of Conservation, and from my thirty-eight years of hunting and fishing around the Allagash.

This volume's first narrative, *Carl a Wise Old Canoe,* evolved from stories told to me by people like Allagash Ranger Lee Hafford and his wife, historian and teacher Faye Hafford. Natives of Allagash Village the Haffords are an encyclopedia of the natural history and folklore of the area.

The second chronicle, *Oscar the Awkward Osprey,* is based on an event that my family and I saw while canoeing across one of the Allagash lakes. That particular day the water's surface was mirror calm, the reflected shoreline images cracked only by the forward motion of our canoe. All of a sudden an osprey, flying from behind us, swooped down and skimmed off the water, bouncing off the surface several times like a skipping stone, until he was on the other side of the lake. The bird reminded us of how a feathered creature might act if it had an itch on its belly that it couldn't quite reach, but desperately needed to scratch.

The last yarn, *Attack at Partridge Junction*, grew from a bird-hunting trip with a friend and his grandchildren. We had spent most of one October day looking for the elusive game bird. Among brilliant reds, yellows and oranges of the fall foliage, we had traveled and walked for miles in the crisp air looking for the delicacy to add to our supper plate. As daylight waned we headed back to the camp, disappointed that we had not seen more birds. Even our golden retriever looked sad and depressed at the lack of action. As we drove around a corner in the road, our minds more concerned with supper than with hunting; when suddenly a partridge appeared beside the road, as if by magic. Like a specter the apparition shimmered into focus, appearing out of nowhere. The bird was very, very quiet as it searched for its evening meal.

Immediately the truck was brought to a halt and the young grandson anxiously climbed out to finally get his bird. The partridge, sensing immediate danger, straightened out his neck to get a better look for any potential threat. Then in confusion it began running, but not flying away as is their usual habit; the biddy actually darted at the young hunter. The boy, surprised by the bird's actions, raised his shotgun and fired too quickly. He missed his target. To those of us watching from the pickup, it looked like the bird had made up its mind to fight his way out of danger.

These stories, while fiction, involve real people and places and include escapades that anyone might experience in the Maine woods. I hope you enjoy reading them as much as we have enjoyed bringing them to you.

Tim Caverly

Millinocket, Maine

October 2010

LET THE "TAILS" BEGIN!

Student Artwork by Mike DiBona

CARL'S ALLAGASH JOURNEY

Carl's Allagash Journey

(It's early May and the sunny days of spring have finally broken the icy grip of a frigid Maine winter. After a long hibernation, a wise old canoe is returning to the North Maine Woods to visit with his friends.)

Ohhh! Groans Carl! *I need to be taken off this canoe rack. I can't believe the roads to the Allagash* **williwags** *are so rough. My ribs are killing me, and it feels like my back is about to break. Bouncing over these never-ending potholes on the back of this rattletrap truck have* **slackened** *all my* **tie-downs**! *I've jounced around so much that it feels like all of my nails, bolts, and screws are loose... ouch, I hurt! I can't wait to get to the river; I've been on the back of this old rig way toooo long!*

Even though he is tired, spring is a thrilling time for Carl. After a whole winter of being on vacation, he is returning to work and Carl is very proud of his **occupation**. You see, it is his job to carry people and their gear along rivers and streams in the state's remote forests. That's because Carl is a twenty-foot green canoe. More specifically, he is a proud Guide's model watercraft made by the Old Town Canoe Company, and Carl loves to float the Allagash. Even though the canoe has been paddled down a number of the state's rivers, he finds something mystical about the state's only **designated** National **Wild and Scenic River**. Carl gets so excited every time he returns with his friend Gil the guide, that it is just like he's exploring this remote northwest corner of the state for the very first time.

Normally Carl feels pretty good, except this time the long hours of being carried on the back of a truck over washed out, dusty, gravel roads have left him stiff and sore. But his discomfort is only temporary. Carl knows that once he senses the power of the water's current under his **keel**, he will feel as refreshed as you or I when we have a drink of cold spring water on a **sweltering** summer day.

It has been six whole months since the canoe and his Maine guide have traveled their favorite stretch of the Allagash and, as the pair approaches the river, the smell from a young thicket of fir trees reminds them of the aroma of Christmas. This time, the team has **sojourned** into the woods as part of a three-day scouting trip in preparation for the upcoming canoeing season. Greeted by alder leaves as big as a mouse's ear, and the unfurling **fronds** of the **fiddlehead**, Carl and Gil arrive at the **put-in** at upper Allagash Stream. Carl is anxious to see if there have been any changes along the river. After months of separation, he is all a-**twitter** to see his Allagash acquaintances.

When it comes time to clean up, where is she? I'll tell you where! She's off gallivanting.

On the Water

While Gil visits campsites and checks for **snags** in the river channel, Carl stretches to work out his kinks, and washes the dust off his canvas covering. After only a few minutes of being paddled, Carl sees something moving in the distance. As he draws closer, he recognizes that it's his old crony, Flat Tail the beaver. The rodent has climbed on top of a log beside his house and is sitting in the sun grumbling and mumbling. Carl hollers, "What's the matter, old pal? You sound **exasperated**!"

"I am busier than ants at a picnic!" Says an annoyed Flat Tail. "And that long skinny-tailed varmint of a neighbor just keeps making more work for me."

"Who do you mean?" asks Carl as he raises his eyebrows **inquisitively**.

The beaver was so mad that he ignored the question and continued to **rant**. "I am trying to get my spring cleaning done and she just keeps packing my freshly scrubbed house with grass, weeds and clamshells. Arrrrgghhh! That **vixen** always wants to share my house, but then she goes and fills it with all sorts of rubble. Then when it comes time to clean up, where is she? I'll tell you where! She's off **gallivanting**. This time that little spitfire has made one mess too many; I am sick and tired of cleaning up after her! I've got *sooo* much stuff to do!!"

"Are you talking about Suzy the Muskrat?" inquired Carl.

"You can call her Suzy if you want to! I call her a poor excuse for a neighbor," growled Flat Tail. "Why, just this morning I found a half eaten **chub** in my living room. And that's not the worst of it! Now with the warmer weather of spring, she is shedding her winter coat. Her fur is all over the place and it's making me… ahhh-chooo! … sneeze." Quickly Flat Tail wipes his nose with the back of a furry foot and threatens, "If she doesn't start picking up after herself, I am going to throw all her stuff outside and relocate my whole kit and caboodle down…ahhh-chooo! ...stream. Oh how I hate allergies!"

Carl's eyes crinkled with amusement because he knew that both muskrats and beavers had beautiful, **lustrous** pelts that kept them warm and dry. And he wasn't sure if there was much difference between the two skins, at least as far as causing an allergic reaction was concerned. Carl also knew that Flat Tail's warning to kick Suzy out of his hut was a silly idea. The beaver and muskrat were actually the best of friends, and they had shared Flat Tail's lodge longer than Carl could remember. Even so, Carl humored Flat Tail by saying, "All in all, your lodge would be a proud home for any animal." Then, to calm the beaver, the canoe cleverly changed the subject by asking, "By the way, how is your cousin Charlie?"

"Why, thank you Carl, I work hard to keep fresh **alders** woven into my lodge," beamed Flat Tail. "You always have a good word to say that brightens my day. And yes, Charlie is doing very well, thank you for asking. In fact, just last week he helped some canoers who almost wrecked in **Chase Rapids**. It's too bad he's cross-eyed and narrow-tailed. Charlie is such a nice fellow."

As Carl floated away, Flat Tail hollered, "Hey, keep an eye out for fresh poplar branches for me-they are very tender this time of year.

"Caaarl," Flat Tail's voice continued to follow, "don't forget about the bend in the river just below the rapids, there's usually a spruce **sweeper** in the river channel."

"Oh, yes! I remember it now!" brightened Carl, "I'll be on the **lookout**."

Boy, Carl thought, as they continued floating downstream, *I am sure glad that Gil tightened my loose joints before putting me into the water-I feel just like a brand new canoe. I am especially happy for the support of my **thwarts**. They are important not only because they keep me strong in the flow of the river, but because the guide also uses them, with a **yoke**, to carry me on **portages**. My partner and I have a nice arrangement. In the river, I carry him, and on land, he carries me. We* *make a good team!*

Flat Tail's warning had reminded Carl of an old canoeing **adage**:

Jeepers, creepers, keep your peepers pealed
on the river's bend.
Jeepers, creepers, keep your peepers pealed
for that tree's end;
Those branches might grab,
and over you'll tip
Smack into the water,
the end of your trip!

Just then, Carl saw a tree lying diagonally across the river channel, directly in front of them. *Oh no! It was the sweeper that Flat Tail had warned about!* panicked Carl.

Here, a deep and powerful current forced the canoe toward the partially submerged tree. The craft was being drawn against its will, as if invisible hands were pulling it closer and closer to being devoured by a demon of the deep. The churning water boiled, rolled and rumbled against the side of the vessel as it pitched dangerously close to swamping. Gil quickly braced his feet against the bottom of the canoe and planted the canoe pole deep into the riverbed. His muscles grew **taut** as he jabbed the pole to snub Carl away from the danger. The scraggly cold fingers of the tree's branches bobbed and gurgled in the water as the boughs reached out for their prey. At the last possible moment, the guide swung the bow with the flow of the current so that the canoe's bow slipped around the downstream end of the tree. The watery branches disappointedly brushed against Carl's side as he swiftly glided by.

Sundown, the First Day

Oh, what a nice time we've had today! reflected Carl as he was poled to the landing at the Little Allagash Falls Campsite on Round Pond. All day Gil and Carl had watched wildlife as the canoe was paddled and poled downstream. They had seen deer, moose, loons, and even glimpsed Oscar the Osprey belly waumpin. Gil and his canoe had blended quietly as one with the river community, respecting the home of their wildlife friends. The twinkling of the evening star signaled that it was nearly time for bed and the red sunset slowly melted into a velvet twilight.

When they got close to shore Gil stepped into the water and, so as not to scratch the canoe's bottom on the rocks, picked up Carl by the bow and carried him onto the beach.

After being unloaded, Carl was turned upside down near the campsite to protect him for the night. Soon, Gil had a campfire built, and the air was filled with the aroma of cedar wood smoke and boiling coffee. Carl drifted off to sleep to the lullaby of the whispering pine, as its swaying branches cradled the night **yodel** of the loon.

Dawn, the Second Day

Early the next morning, Carl was awakened by the sound of laughter. It wasn't a light chuckle either, but the kind of hearty roar that comes from deep down in the belly. It was a body-shaking, side-splitting, eye-watering, horse laugh. Carl looked around and saw that it was Billy the Black Bear who was raising such a ruckus. In fact, Billy was laughing so hard that he was curled on his back with his legs in the air. The bear was holding his back paws by his front paws, hysterically rocking back and forth.

"What in the world...?" Carl curiously muttered to himself.

When Billy realized that Carl was there he rolled into a sitting position and snickered, "You should... hee, hee, ha, ha! You should have ha, ha, ha, ha. You should have seen what I just saw," the bear said as he wiped the tears from his eyes. Hearty laughter such as Billy's is catching, so Carl giggled and asked, "Hee, hee, hee, what was it?"

"Why," explained Billy, "I just saw Thelma; you must remember Thelma, the bushy tailed red squirrel?"

Before Carl could respond Billy continued, "Well, she was trying to swim across the thoroughfare, ha ha hee hee. Each time she'd get halfway across Teddy Trout, thinking the squirrel's tail was a big mayfly, would jump and nip at it. When Thelma felt something tugging on her tail, she would get frightened and head back to the shore from where she had started. The fourth time that squirrel swam across the narrows; she was holding the end of her tail in her mouth to keep it from being bitten. Well by gosh, finally she made it all the way across with out being bothered again! Although, her tail did look like it was a couple of inches shorter than it had been. You should have heard the sassy chattering that Thelma gave Teddy after she climbed to the safety of the black spruce that's behind Gil's tent! The squirrel was very embarrassed because she knows that brook trout can't keep a secret and her escapade would be spread throughout the woods!"

"Ha, ha, ha." Carl joined in on the laughter as he imagined the silly sight. The canoe also knew that because trout traveled in schools, the fish would spread the story far and wide to every lake and stream in the north country. Carl remembered advice from an old woodsman, *if you wanna keep a secret, then don't tell a trout.*

Billy waddled off shaking his head and giggling, "Swimming with her tail in her mouth, ha, ha, hee, hee, hee." Then he looked back over his shoulder and hollered, "Glad to see you back out on the water again my friend."

Carl smiled to himself and thought, *Billy has such a great sense of humor, he is so much fun to be around.*

Carl and Gil spent the rest of that day on the water exploring and enjoying nature as only a person and canoe can do. That night, they fell asleep under a watchful moon, as a murmuring spring breeze kept the humming mosquitoes at bay.

Last Day of the Scouting Trip

On the third day at the Outlet Campsite, Gil woke early to get a good start before the wind picked up on Allagash Lake. Serenaded by the *Po-or Sam Peabody, Peabody, Peabody* call of the white-throated sparrow, the guide dined on a quick breakfast of coffee, and pancakes sprinkled with sweet field strawberries and maple syrup. As the camping gear was stored into Carl, the bow of the canoe waited patiently on the cobblestone beach while it's stern was gently rocked by the morning waves. Carl, only partially awake, drowsily **contemplated** what the day would bring. Suddenly, a feathered brown cyclone burst out from under a little fir tree. With the fury of a tornado, the brown whirlwind was a spinning mass of wings and spiked toes headed directly for Gil. But the nimble woodsman swiftly sidestepped the mass of exploding plumage. It was a partridge that was as mad as mad could be. The bird landed on the ground only a short distance from Carl and started strutting that "don't mess with me" walk. Immediately, the canoe recognized the attacker as Penny the ruffed grouse. He could see that something had upset the bird so badly that her dark ruffed neck feathers were raised; a sure sign of anger from what is normally a gentle creature. A troubled Carl asked, "Why, Penny what's the matter? I've never seen you so **aggressive**!"

The irritated bird answered sharply, "You'd be upset too if someone nearly stepped on your babies!"

"Huh?" quizzed Carl.

"I have a brood of 10 of the prettiest buff colored eggs you've ever seen. And if I hadn't acted, the way I did, that clodhopper was going to step on em."

As Carl listened, his stern continued to bob in the waves washing onto shore. "I'm glad you were able to prevent Gil from hurting them. In his rush to get on the water, he must not have seen you sitting on the nest. Gil would never intentionally hurt any of his Allagash friends."

"I am not so sure. After all it's my family at stake, you know! Why, just a few minutes ago, one of my chicks used his egg tooth to break through his shell." Penny held her head high as she proudly added, "and he has his father's eyes." Without any further ado the hen continued, "I am going to do my broken wing act in order to lead the man away from my babies."

With that, Penny limped away, crying the most pitiful cry; one would make even the coldest person's heart bleed. The bird was dragging one wing as if she were the easiest catch there could ever be. Gil was experienced in the ways of the woods, so he ignored Penny's act, knelt carefully on one knee and lifted the lower branches of a nearby fir seedling. He found the nest that the mother was trying to protect. Gil turned to the bird and said, "Don't worry girl I am not going to hurt your babies. I'll leave as soon as Carl is loaded with our camping equipment." Within minutes, as Gil pushed Carl from shore, the canoe could hear the father partridge drumming on a hollow log behind the campsite, and he knew that Penny and her family were going to be all right.

Late Afternoon, the Same Day

It was the last day of the trip, and Carl had been poled back upstream to the pickup. While the canoe was waiting to be unloaded, he heard a series of soft thuds. They sounded like wet sponges being thrown onto the ground. Carl looked up to see a large bird with a black head with a bright red crest. He immediately recognized his friend Wally the **Pileated** (pill-ee-ate-ed) **Woodpecker.** Wally was trying to drill a hole in a tree, as he selected insects to eat in a north woods **buffet**.

"Hello, Wally!" hollered Carl.

"Hey, what! Who's there? Whyth, hallo, Carl," lisped a startled Wally. As the bird turned to look at the canoe, Carl noticed that Wally had a strange stuffed up sound to his voice. Similar to you or I when we are sick with a cold.

"You sound funny, Wally. Do you have a beak cold?", asked Carl.

"Tho, but I wish I did," answered Wally. "I have thomething that is much, much worthe."

"What could that possibly be?", asked a worried Carl.

"Do you wemember dat old logging camp over on the Saint Juste Road?"

"The one with the tin roofs?" **queried** Carl.

"Yeth," exhaled Wally. "Thast week I was thumming on the roof to thisten to the thound. You know

33

how good it thounds? It'th muthic to my ears. Well the camp **caretaker** pinned a pieth of thalt pork on the clothethline for me."

"That was nice of him," remarked Carl.

"I thought tho too... at the time, " moaned Wally. "I tharted pecking on that thalt pork thinking that he wath feeding me ath a reward for the beautiful muthic I made. Well, as fath as I would eat a piethe, he would bring out another. It wath real good. After thixth pietheth of pork, he thopped putting it out. I wanted more, tho I went back to pecking on the tin roof. Wouldn't you know that pork made my beak tho thoft that when I pecked on the tin I couldn't make a thound. Now ith'th ethtwemely hard for me to eat. Ith's juth ath if my beak ith made out of rubber. Every time I try to peck the bark of a juithy bug filled tree, my beak juth bendth and bountheth off"

"Well, wouldn't that frost ya Wally!" exclaimed Carl. "I can remember when your beak would hit a tree so hard it sounded like a steel hammer hitting a solid wooden plank. Not like a wet noodle slapping a piece of paper, as it sounds now. I would hate to have that happen to me. You must be extremely hungry!"

Before Wally could answer Carl remembered, "If it is any help, I saw a half-rotten pine stump just around the bend, and it was crawling with carpenter ants and beetles."

"Thankth, Carl," lisped Wally as he flew off. "I am juth about tharrved. You will be my bethth friend forever."

By now the canoe was completely unloaded and had been placed on the canoe rack of the truck. As the truck started down the dusty road Carl felt sad to be leaving the Allagash River. But then he smiled because he remembered that they would be back soon. Maybe the next time they would see the Allagash ranger, his little girl and their golden retriever, patrolling as he knew they liked to do.

This story has received the Misty the Golden Retriever,

"*Contented Sigh of Approval*".

Oscar the Awkward Osprey

Student Artwork by Joshua Perrotti

Oscar the Awkward Osprey

(An Allagash Belly Waumpin')

(The canoe shudders because the outboard motor is forcing the craft upstream against the raging current of the powerful river. As the sun reclines on the shoulders of the western horizon, a Ranger and his ten-year-old daughter are returning from a day's patrol on a remote river in northern Maine. They have been traveling since early morning, and are headed home after visiting Round Pond in **Township 13**, **Range 12 WELS***. Sitting low in the bow, the daughter watches for rocks as the canoeman expertly pilots his craft in a switchback fashion, following the twisting channel of the river.*

All day a heavy prevailing wind has churned the water into frothing **whitecaps***, until the liquid surfaces resemble a whipped topping. After portaging over Long Lake Dam, the two travelers are relieved to see that the northwest gusts have finally died. The pond behind the dam has become smooth, like a mirror, reflecting the images of the* **coniferous** *forest hugging its shore.*

Continuing up Long Lake, smack dab in the middle

of the Allagash Wilderness Waterway, the voyagers smile as they watch nature's playground unfold before them. On a distant hillside the pink and purple blossoms of the wild **lupine** and fireweed silhouette a bull moose standing up to its **haunches** in water, contentedly munching on delicate plants. A deer and her spotted fawn are wading along the shore. Every once in a while the mother raises her head and licks the air, testing for signs of danger, only to drop her head and nip off a tasty bud of a wild rose bush. Overhead, the whistling wings of a common goldeneye duck alerts her neighbors that it's nearly time for bed.

Propelled along, the wayfarers watch trout roll to the surface of the lake, the fish briefly exposing their pink bellies as they attempt to capture an evening **mayfly**. As the father and daughter near Grey Book Campsite, a tenting party waves a hearty hello and invites in a loud voice, "Stop in. You're just in time for fresh coffee, hot chocolate, and banana boats."

The ranger waves and cuts the outboard to swing into shore. As the canoe comes about, the craft's keel slices through the ripples caused by the fish rising all around them. The man uses a **canoe pole** to snub their

speed, and the wake from the motor lifts the crafts bow and gently sets it onto the beach. The large canoe barely makes a sound as it halts on the pea gravel.

After a brief greeting, and conversation about water levels in the river, coffee is poured and the group relaxes in front of the campfire. One of the campers says, "Earlier today we saw a large bird flying along and every once in a while he would drop and bounce off the lake. "What was he doing? Could the bird have been sick?" Excitedly the daughter blurts out, "Oh that was Oscar!" " Then she turns to her father and pleads in that little girl voice, "Tell em about Oscar, Daddy, please?"

"All right munch," answers her dad, affectionately using his daughter's nickname. So the ranger begins...)

"Well...no, the bird wasn't sick. What you witnessed was Oscar, belly waumpin. Its a fairly common occurrence around these parts," the outdoorsman assures the campers. The man behind the badge then asks his audience, "Have you ever done anything that was so much fun that it made you happier than a gopher digging in soft dirt? Something that was so enjoyable, you laughed as hard as a raccoon that had just discovered a ripe cornfield? An experience that brought you so much pleasure, your face beamed as if you'd just been told you could have all of the ice cream and chocolate candy that you wanted?" The members of his captive audience nod in agreement as each one recalls a treasured memory.

"Well folks, that's how Oscar feels about belly waumpin. In fact, he loves it so much he would just die to belly waump. And that's all there is to it! Whenever Oscar thinks about belly waumpin, he begins to grin, tee-hee and giggle, and he continues to laugh all the time he is doing it."

A camper, spellbound and hanging onto the rangers every word ask, "Exactly who is Oscar, and what's belly waumpin?"

Caught up in the story the ranger's daughter eagerly interrupts, "Oscar is one of our favorite Allagash characters."

"That's right," continues her father. "You see Oscar is a proud bird of **prey** called an osprey. He lives just upstream from here on Umsaskis Lake near the Ledges Campsite. Oscar is a handsome bird that weighs about four pounds. There is a mask over his eyes that, when you first see him, remind you of wrap around sunglasses. The bird is a graceful flyer who has arched wings with four finger like tips angled slightly backwards, and he loves living on the Allagash."

A second camper asks, "Okay, so…what does belly waumpin have to do with Oscar?

" In good time, in good time," the ranger answers, smiling as he unhurriedly weaves his fable. "Well, it is an unusual story, but if everyone insists on hearing it, may I have another cup of coffee with honey? It is quite a tale that I have to tell."

Coffee cups are refilled and the storyteller continues. "Well sir, it all started several years ago. One day at dawn, Oscar decided to go fishing. Now you need to understand that Oscar doesn't fish like we do. He doesn't have any need for fishing poles, lines, sinkers, or worms. That's because Oscar fishes with his feet.

It was one of those lazy, hot, cloudless, summer, **katydid** days in the Maine woods. All was in harmony along the river. Wally the woodpecker was pecking for insects in an old pine tree, Charles the narrow tailed beaver was putting fresh mud on his lodge, and keeping an eye out for stranded canoeists. Marvin the merganser was swimming sluggishly near shore with his head under water looking for an easy meal. The day was so perfect the osprey couldn't have anticipated the change that was coming to his world.

Now Oscar really likes to eat fish; I mean he really likes to eat fish! In fact he is so fond of his favorite food that sometimes he will eat as much as his own weight of the delicacy in a single day. Almost as much as eating, Oscar likes to catch fish. He will ride the **air thermals**, spiraling higher and higher over a lake or river for hours, patiently waiting and watching for that silver flash of a trout as it rises to feeds on flies. When he sees a fish, Oscar straightens his feet, opens his toes, folds his wings, then faster than lightning plunges into the lake, grabbing the fish with his sharp **talons**. If he is flying a long way to a perch or nest, Oscar will use his feet to turn the trout in midair so the fish's head faces forward."

"Why does he do that?" A woman asks as she pokes at the campfire with a long stick and sends a shower of red sparks into the cool twilight air.
"It **aerodynamics**," the naturalist replies. "Turning the fish so its head faces forward reduces the air drag caused by his heavy lunch so Oscar doesn't have to work so hard
46

flapping his wings."

"Then," the woodsman continues, "holding tightly onto his treasure, the bird flies to a nearby tree limb to eat his snack. Now Oscar understands that there aren't as many trout as there used to be. So once in a while he thinks it might be nice to catch and release a few. But you must know how good raw fish taste. Once Oscar has caught one, his beak starts watering and quicker than a bear going to honey, he is sitting on a tree limb in the sun, with a full belly, **preening** his feathers. To an Osprey, raw fish is as good a meal as any Thanksgiving feast that you or I could imagine. Doesn't such a fine meal make your mouth water too?" the man asked grinning, and winking at his daughter.

Another woman smiles and jokes, "you mean the brook trout is like wilderness **sushi** for wildlife?"

"I suppose," nods the ranger. "Anyway, one particular day Oscar was riding updrafts, fishing, when he spied an especially fat brook trout. With his beak already starting to water, Oscar climbed very high so he could **plunge** and seize the prize with blinding speed. But just as he folded his wings and started to drop, the trout spied Oscar and raced to deep water and to hide under a

submerged log. Oscar, in the middle of his lunge, tried to adjust his dive, but he was going too fast. He ended up overshooting the fish, and skimmed along on the water totally missing the trout. The feathers on his belly made a *waump waump* sound as he awkwardly bounced along the lake on his stomach. If you were in a canoe a long way away, you might think that someone had skipped a giant rock along the surface of a pond.

Shaking the water from his wings, and climbing back towards the sky, Oscar's cheek feathers turned red with embarrassment. He had hit the water at such an angle that he skidded along the top of the lake. He had never missed a fish before. He certainly had never skipped across the surface of a lake before. *Oh I hope no one saw me!* Fretted Oscar."

"Yet at the same time Oscar had felt a strange tingling sensation in his belly! He had never felt anything so unusual and yet so good at the same time. *Hmm,* Oscar thought, as he looked around to see if anyone had been watching, *maybe I should try that again?* So Oscar spiraled high into the air, folded his wings, shifted his weight and fell at a slant towards Umsaskis Lake. And guess what? He bounced right off the lake and back into the air. Again it tickled his belly. In fact it tickled him enough to make him laugh right out loud. After a couple of days of practice, Oscar got so good at skipping along the water, or belly waumpin, as he liked to call it, he could skim whenever he wanted. He learned that if he was careful with the angle of his fall, Oscar could start at one side of Umsaskis and belly waump all the way across the lake without having to stop to rest. Oscar thought, *next to catching fish, this is the most fun I've ever had. I think I'll do it again.*

So tomorrow, as you continue your trip, watch for an osprey soaring overhead. If you suddenly hear the bird giggle and see it abruptly drop at a slant out of the sky and belly waump, wave a big hello to Oscar."

With that the Ranger announces that due to the coming darkness, it was time for them to continue their journey. The campers thanked the ranger and daughter for stopping and invited the couple to visit again. The ranger says they would, and promised "next time I'll show you how to roast a watermelon." The father and little girl bid their new friends a pleasant **bon soir**, started the canoe's outboard motor and slowly followed a watery moonlight path towards their wilderness cabin.

his story has received a *Purr of Approval* from Sam the

Cat.

(Sam likes any story that has to do with birds)

Attack At Partridge Junction

Student Artwork by Travis Hartley

Attack

At Partridge
Junction

Attack At Partridge Junction

Alayna and Preston lie in their beds and whispered excitedly. The youngsters were still wide awake even though their grandmother had hollered several times from the foot of the stairs leading up to their rooms. "You children stop talking now and go to sleep, tomorrow is going to be a very long day!" But Gram's warnings only caused them to stick their heads under their pillows and lower their voices to a soft murmur. The two youngsters were too stirred up to sleep.

Tomorrow would be Thursday and the children already knew that they were going to be spending a lot of time riding. However, tonight they were staying at their grandparent's big old log cabin in preparation for an early start in the morning. Their vehicle was all packed and sleeping bags had been stored in waterproof bags so the gang could get on the road early. The kids would be leaving at the crack of dawn with their grandfather to drive to a distant corner of Maine called the Allagash for a bird-hunting trip. The young adventurers had been told that this part of the state held a vast forest; the exploration possibilities seemed endless.

But realizing that they were going to be so far from home for such a long time also gave them cold chills. There really wasn't any reason for their nervousness because they were going to be with their grandfather and Preston's father, yet! They felt an unexplainable uneasiness. Little could the children predict what was about to happen? If they had only known how terrifying the experience would become; they would never have left home!

Early Friday morning they woke to the sounds of pots and pans rattling in a faraway kitchen as the smell of an early morning breakfast filled the air. The aroma of frying bacon, boiling coffee and homemade baked beans teased their noses. As the pair labored to rise, they struggled to shake the sleep cobwebs from their heads. *This isn't our bedroom, it can't be! We aren't snuggled in our comfy beds, under homemade quilts. There aren't any sports posters of the Celtics and Red Sox covering their walls. And Mom isn't hollering, "Hurry now, it's time to get up for school. The bus is coming and you don't want to be late."*

Instead, they found themselves wrapped in tightly zipped sleeping bags, lying on narrow cots with lumpy pillows that smelled of wood smoke, **perspiration** and **Old Woodsman Fly Dope**. *Where are we?* The children wondered as they rolled over and struggled to find the zipper of their twisted bedrolls, then they remembered...

Oh yes, yesterday! Our grandfather took us out of school for an **excursion** *into the remote North Woods of Maine. It was October and we had left home to hunt partridge with two friends and Misty, the Golden Retriever. But now it was time to rise and shine.*

Jumping out of bed, their bare feet hit the cold, gray painted plywood floor. Misty greeted each one, licking first one face, and then the other. With the waving flag of the dog's tail leading the way, the two made their way towards the massive kitchen and breakfast.

The adventure had really started several days before, when they began planning for the journey. In preparation for the trip their grandfather (called Papa) and Preston's father Eddie had pored over maps. With the turning of every page of their Delorme's Atlas the adults pointed to places with strange sounding names like Umbazookus, Chesuncook, and Caucomgonoc Lakes that were hundreds of miles away. They were going to pass by such places as the Ice Caves, Allagash Mountain and

Ciss Stream. On the way to their borrowed abode they would cross a wood-harvesting route ominously called the "Deadman Road." And just a couple of ridges over, Papa promised, were two abandoned locomotives, or ghosts trains that maybe they could hike into by using a compass.

Questions flooded their minds as they helped to pack everything needed to travel far from their Dennysville home in Washington County to the remote Allagash woods. In turn the kids asked dozens of questions, "How far is it? How long will it take to get there? Will there be anyone else there?" The children shouted in unison, ending with the question, "Should we bring our favorite movie?"

Papa replied, "It is a long drive so you have to be patient. And he sternly reminded, "No squabbling! There may be a few people around, but we won't see very many, and no, you do not need to take your movies. There won't be any way to watch them."

When the day finally came to leave, twelve-year-old Alayna and ten-year-old Preston decided they were too excited to be sad about leaving their mother and sisters behind. For hours the crew drove northwest from their coastal Maine town, diagonally traversing closer and closer towards Maine's dark forest. After passing the giant mill in Baileyville, through the small town of Topsfield, and watching the sun reflect off the cool water of the West Branch of the Penobscot River, they arrived at Millinocket. A mill town that at one time was renown for its papermaking, now recognized as the gateway to majestic Mt. Katahdin and beyond. Driving up the Golden road the purple mountain seemed to back away from the group as if warning, "your going too far into the woods, turn back, turn back now." Riding on dirt roads for what seemed forever, they finally reached the old camp where they would be staying for the next three days.

The cabin was a tin roofed, green-**asphalt**-sided, porcupine-chewed drafty old building, an odd looking structure. It could hardly be called a shelter, and large limbs from giant pine trees hovered over the roof like a vulture getting ready to pounce on fresh prey.

Rusted hinges of the old bedroom door groaned in protest at being forced open to allow in fresh air. Walking inside, the first thing Alayna and Preston noticed was that the rooms didn't have any electricity, running water, or even a refrigerator. Looking around at the lack of conveniences, the children silently gulped as it sunk in that the nearest gas station, McDonalds, and doctor were over a hundred miles away. They were completely on their own. This was going to be a real adventure, a true test of their outdoor survival skills!

Once inside they saw that the building wasn't really a cabin like the rounded log ones at home, but a big old lumber camp that had been built in the shape of a huge lazy n. The kitchen was at the foot of the left leg; the washroom and more beds were in the middle, and a large bedroom with fourteen cots was in the right leg.

Bolted over each window were two-rusted **crosscut saw blades** used to prevent varmints from breaking the windows and entering the camp. Here Papa emphasized, as if the family would have to protect their own cottage in the same way someday, *always install two blades, one at the top of the window and one at bottom about ten inches apart. The teeth of the saw blades need to point at each other to prevent bears from getting in.*

Alayna and Preston also saw evidence that the historic building had been used for many years as a woods camp. In the kitchen there were enough benches and long tables to seat at least fifty men. Dominant in the room was the elephant size gas range, big enough to feed an army. The kids could almost smell the sugar pies, chocolate cakes, and mincemeat cookies that must have been baked in the oven of the old black cook stove. Tacked on the walls were old maps that oddly didn't show any roads, only river routes. In the bedroom there was a huge cast iron woodstove Eddie called a **ram down**.

A faded white sign with black letters, "Great Northern Paper," was nailed over the inside door of the bedroom. All the furniture was marked with the letters "GNP" to show that it had once been paper company property. Throughout the camp Alayna and Preston saw what looked like little holes all over the floors. What could have caused them? The holes didn't look like anything that mice or squirrels would have made! Their grandfather explained that caulk boots caused the holes. Caulk boots were footwear with little metal spikes in the soles, made especially for lumberjacks to use during river drives to allow firm footing on wet logs.

That night as a roaring wood stove warmed the room under the yellow din of gaslights; Preston and Alayna tiredly snuggled deep into their sleeping bags. Through the cabin's windows they watched the panoramic display of nature's fireworks, the **northern lights**. Drifting off to sleep with a faded smell of wet wool and tree pitch, they sensed a "movement in the room." Phantom lumberjacks of long ago seemed to be returning home from a typical daylight to dark workday in snapping cold temperatures when steel blades chipped away at frozen trees. The wind blowing outside the thin windows moaned to the children long ago tales about river drives, tote roads, and steaming work horses.

The next morning, after fueling up on a huge breakfast of juice, bacon, eggs, hash browns, beans and toast, it was time for the hunt. Excitedly they crowded into the truck with Misty riding between them. Within an hour both kids had seen and shot at birds. In fact, Alayna had shot at one bird four times, but the partridge was **impervious** to the pellets and flew off. As it flew away, the bird looked back at Alayna with an angry cold **glint** in its eye. *But no!* It must be her imagination because she knew that birds did not show expression, angry or otherwise. Alayna was amazed that she missed the bird; she was a good shot and had always gotten partridge before. But she kept her feelings to herself.

Then it was Preston's turn. After driving a short distance, the kids and the grandfather saw another partridge feeding beside the road, and Papa jammed on the brakes. No one really knew who saw the bird first-Preston, Alayna, Papa or Misty the dog. You see Misty liked to hunt birds so much that she rode with her head on Alayna's or Preston's shoulder, looking through the windshield. When Misty saw a bird, she would stare intently at it, alerting the others that there was one nearby.

After the truck skidded to a halt, Preston eased out of the side door. Walking as quietly as a deer on moss, he crept up on the bird. As soon as he was within range, the young hunter raised his gun and slipped off the safety... but at the same time the bird sensed the intrusion to his feeding ground and he flushed. The boy swung his shotgun, with Papa's words ringing in his ears, *now keep your head down, look through the sight and squeeze slowly, not pull, but slowly squeeeeeze the trigger, Buddy.* The smell of gun smoke was in the air and the bird fell into the thick alder underbrush off to the side of the road. In a flash Misty was out of the truck and had retrieved the bird from it's briar patch bed of tangled blackberry bushes and fireweed. Then it was Alayna's turn. In a short time Misty had retrieved a bird for her as well.

As they drove on, Papa pointed out game crossings, majestic moose, **gorbies**, and red tailed hawks. They glimpsed deer, coyotes, spruce grouse, and the children were awed at the seemingly endless forest. Unfortunately, partridge were nowhere to be seen. It was as if the birds had disappeared. Where could they have gone? Papa couldn't find birds anywhere. There weren't any birds by the streams, in the grass along the sides of the roads, or on the beechnut ridges. The hunters drove and walked old tote roads for miles. But there wasn't a feather to be found. Was it possible the birds had left?

At twilight after hours of driving, retelling old jokes, and eating tons of mini candies, they were tired, and ready for a proper supper. Then, when they got within ten miles of camp and had given up hope of seeing a bird, a partridge softly appeared in the grass along the shoulder of the road, as a ghost rising through a foggy blanket.

Attack!

Papa pulled the truck off to the side of the road, and Preston jumped out to shoot the bird. He swiftly loaded his gun and raised it to take aim. Wait! There was more than one bird. Preston saw a second, then a third, and even more. Alayna hollered, "Hey, watch it-there's a whole **covey**!" Not to be outdone, the girl followed the young boy out of the truck; surely there were enough birds for both of them to get their limit. Preston wanted to get at least one **biddy** before the birds got away and, more important, before Alayna could shoot hers. But which one should he take first? There were so many to choose from.

However, the birds were not flying away as they normally did. In fact, they seemed to be getting into **formation,** and then began running toward the two young hunters. Papa hollered, "Get into the truck quick kids-there is something wrong! The feathered horde is attacking!"

In defense, Preston quickly shot at the first bird. But he jerked the trigger and fired too fast. The lead pellets missed their target. As the birds continued to close in, the kids started backing up toward the truck. But the birds were coming on fast. The kids turned to run, watching their attackers over their shoulders. Preston dropped his gun in fright, and scurried as fast as he could. But the birds were gaining! Alayna's and Preston's feet felt as heavy as if they were wearing lead sneakers. They felt like they were moving in slow motion.

Leading the flock was a ragged looking bird that had a bandage on one leg and was running with a limp. The bird also had a cloth patch over an eye, and he seemed to be in charge. Could it be that the lead bird had been shot at before and somehow had received medical attention? They had never heard of wild birds that had learned about being doctors or nurses.

No matter how fast Preston and Alayna ran, the birds came faster. The old bird was squawking orders. The partridges caught up and began pecking at the children's hair, digging at their jackets with sword like toes and beating the kids with their wings. There were so many birds striking Preston and Alayna that they lost sight of Papa and his truck. The kids were caught in a cloud of partridges.

Suddenly Preston and Alayna heard barking and saw Misty running toward them. The dog was biting, jumping and parting the sea of birds and opening a path to the truck. Preston and Alayna saw the dust-covered pickup just ahead. With Misty bringing up the rear, they made a giant leap through the open truck door and slammed it shut behind them. But the birds, sensing victory, wouldn't stop. They continued to attack in a very **organized** and **coordinated** way. The whole flock was on the truck; the vehicle was shaking and rocking back and forth. A side window broke, and Alayna could feel the wind from beating partridge wings in her face.

Then something changed. The wind wasn't coming from beating wings at all, but ...a wagging tail. Alayna had been dreaming, and her screams from the nightmare had awakened the dog. Misty had jumped on her bed to see what was wrong. The dog was playing with a stocking and was wagging her tail in Alayna's face. It was the dog's tail causing the wind. *Thank goodness-it must have only been a dream* Alayna gasped still trembling with fear.

Alayna looked over at Preston and saw he was still sleeping. Papa was cooking breakfast. Still uneasy from her dream, Alayna stumbled out of bed and followed the smell of sizzling bacon toward the kitchen. She

looked back and saw... a... partridge... feather on her pillow. That's strange, she thought. How could that have gotten there? Silently, in deep thought, she wove her way to the comfort of the warm kitchen.

After breakfast they all left to go hunting on an old road they had been told was a good place to explore. As they drove, she saw a bend in the road that looked strangely familiar. It was the junction in her dream! There was a creeping mist flowing over the road, and there was a partridge feeding at the edge of the fog. Wait, it couldn't be, but... didn't that bird have a patch over one eye?

This story has received the Allie the Dog *tail wag of approval*.

Wilderness Journal

The first thing that many do when they journey into the Maine woods is to write down observations in a daybook, diary, or journal. Why do these adventurers feel the need to keep written records of their outdoor experiences?

Most of us take for granted the comforts of running water, automatic heat, electrical appliances, TV or a nearby fast food store. But what if you didn't have all those things? Then it becomes important that you know where to find the necessities of life. Such items as food, clean water, shelter and knowing how to get out of the woods if you become lost, are all things necessary for any wilderness wanderer to survive.

In other words when we have to rely on our own resource to remain safe, it is important to learn from those experiences and to insure that the lessons are not forgotten. That is why many outdoor people maintain a written record of their firsthand knowledge.

Knowing where the fish can be caught, what animals can help and which one's can hurt, understanding which plants can heal when we get sick, or which plants makes us sick when eaten, can make all the difference in our health and how well we can provide aid to others.

Ask anyone that works in the Maine woods and you will find that wilderness rangers, wardens, lumberjacks, guides, and outdoors people of all types keep track of daily occurrences. Similar to recording the steps of a school science experience such things as; weather, animal habits, places to fish, hiking trails, campsites, where dry firewood is found, how to patch a canoe, or even something of interest to tell the folks back home, are all examples of things written in diaries.

The following pages are made available for you to record your own outdoor experiences so that when you become "A Wilderness Ranger" you will be prepared.

Coming Soon-Allagash Tails Volume IV.
Adventures from *A Wilderness Rangers' Journal*

Wilderness Journal Entry

Wilderness Journal Entry

_____

_____

_____

_____

_____

_____

_____

_____

_____

_____

_____

_____

_____

_____

_____

_____

_____

_____

_____

_____

_____

_____

_____

_____

_____

Wilderness Journal Entry

Wilderness Journal Entry

_____

_____

_____

_____

_____

_____

_____

_____

_____

_____

_____

_____

_____

_____

_____

_____

_____

_____

_____

_____

_____

_____

Wilderness Journal Entry

Wilderness Journal Entry

CHARLIE
THE WHITEWATER BEAVER'S
ANNOTATED GLOSSARY

(Read about the adventures of Charlie in *Allagash Tails Vol. 1*)

Adage: A saying or statement that is commonly used.

Aerodynamics: Force exerted by air on flying and windblown bodies.

Aggressive: Overly confident and certain; assertive

Air Thermal: a column of rising air in the Earth's atmosphere. Thermals are created by the uneven heating of the Earth's surface.

Alder: Tree or shrub that normally grows in wetlands.

Asphalt: A mixture of rock or sand blended with refined petroleum; used to surface roads.

Biddy: Female ruffed grouse.

Buffet: Meal at which guests serve themselves.

Canoe Pole: A long pole, usually ten to twelve feet long and about 1 and ½ inches in diameter, used to propel a canoe through shallow water. Also called a setting pole.

Caretaker: A person who looks after buildings or property during the absence of the owner.

Chase Rapids: Five miles of Class II-III rapids on the

Allagash River. The rapids begins at 925 feet above sea level

Chub: Thick fresh water fish, generally not considered edible.

Coniferous: Kind of Softwood, evergreen trees that produce cones.

Coordinate: Arrange in a proper order.

Contemplate: To look at or think about intently.

Covey: A small flock of game birds.

Crosscut Saw: Thin steel saw blade and large saw teeth, used by lumberjacks to cut trees. The blades are generally seventy inches long and seven inches in width. It was made for use by or two people.

Designate: Mark or point out. Identify as special as in "Designated Wild River."

Exasperate: Greatly annoyed, irritated.

Excursion: A short trip taken for interest or pleasure.

Fiddlehead Frond: Edible unfurled leaf of a variety of ferns such as the ostrich fern.

Formation: Way in which something is arranged.

Gallivant: Gad about, going here and there for no particular purpose.

Glint: A gleam or flash.

Gorby: Nickname for a bird known as the Canada Jay. It

lives in coniferous forests.

Haunches: Hips of an animal.

Hibernate: Spend winter in sleep or in an inactive condition.

Impervious: Allowing no passage, not open to argument.

Inquisitive: Curious.

Katydid: Large green grasshopper like insect. Male makes a shrill noise that sounds like its name. Often heard during warm sunny days.

Keel: The part of a canoe or boat that extends along the whole length of the bottom of the craft, normally made of wood or metal.

Lookout: A place that has a commanding a wide view.

Lupine: Colorful wild plant with a long spike of flowers.

Lustrous: Shining, glossy.

Mayfly: Short lived, slender aquatic insect. Favorite food of the brook trout.

Northern Lights: Also known as the *Aurora Borealis.* A natural light display that lights up the northern horizon with a greenish or a faint red spectrum.

Occupation: Work; employment.

Old Woods Men Fly Dope: An old time insect repellent invented in 1882, it was made specifically to repel the persistent

Maine black fly.

Organize: Arrange; put into working order.

Perspiration: Sweat.

Pileated Woodpecker: Large North American woodpecker. Mainly black with red crest on its head.

Plunge: Throw oneself, or be thrown, into the water.

Portage: Carrying a canoe or provisions overland from one lake or river to another.

Preening: The actions of a bird as it smoothes or arranges its feathers with its beak.

Prey: To hunt, or kill for food, or the food that is hunted.

Put-In: Access point to a body of water.

Query: Question; inquiry.

Ram Down: Type of cast iron wood stove, rectangular shaped with hinged cover. Named because top cover could be lifted and large pieces of wood could be forced, shoved or rammed into the firebox.

Rant: Speak wildly; noisily.

Ruffed Grouse: Non-migratory game bird with a plump body and ruffs on both sides of its neck. Found from the Appalachian Mountains across Canada and to Alaska.

Slacken: Make or become loose.

Snag: Tree or branch with one end held fast to the bottom of a river, stream or pond.

Sojourn: A brief stay or visit.

Spiraling: Winding and a gradually winding circle; either upward or downward. Generally describes the upward flight of a bird of prey.

Sushi: Oriental delicacies consisting of fish eaten raw.

Sweeper: A tree or large branch lying partially submerged in the current of a river or stream.

Swelter: Suffer from heat; sweat.

Talons: The claws of a bird of prey.

Taut: Tightly drawn.

Thwart: Brace or support connecting gunwhales of a canoe.

Tie Downs: Rope, nylon cord or similar constriction to confine, or restrict. As in "tie-downs are used to fasten canoes to canoe racks on trucks or canoe trailers.

Township 13 Range 12 WELS: A unit of government for one of Maine's unorganized territories. Townships are six miles square and the number refers to a position of latitude; Range refers to position of longitude; WELS, refers to a designation of "West of the Easterly Line of the State."

Traverse: Pass across an area.

Twitter: To titter; giggle.

Vixen: A woman regarded as quarrelsome, shrewish, or malicious.

Whitecaps: A wave with its crest broken into white foam.

Wild and Scenic River: A designation by the National Park Service that provides a certain level of recognition and protection.

Williwags: Any remote, outlying or far-flung place.

Yodel: Form of singing that uses extended notes.

Yoke: Crossbeams added to canoes to allow them to be carried on shoulders. The supports are shaped to fit over shoulders and around back of neck.

Photo by Larry Michaud

About the Author:
Tim Caverly

Tim has spent his life in Maine's outdoors, growing up in Baxter State Park and Maine's forests. While in college at the University of Maine at Machias, he worked summers for the Maine State Park and Recreation Commission. After graduating with a Bachelor of Science degree, it was natural for him to continue employment with the State of Maine.

In 1999 he retired from Maine's Department of Conservation after assignments at Sebago Lake State Park, as well as manager of Aroostook and Cobscook Bay State Parks. Tim topped off his career with the Department as supervisor of the Allagash Wilderness Waterway, where he and his wife Susan lived for eighteen years.

Tim and Sue currently reside in Millinocket where they are employed by the Millinocket School System. The couple enjoys raising Golden Retrievers, and look forward to sharing more stories about the Allagash.

About the Illustrator:
Franklin Manzo, Jr.

Frank was born and raised in Millinocket, Maine where he attended Stearns High School. He retired to his family homestead after working as a software engineer for over 25 years.

He has since worked as the Editor of a local newspaper, is noted as a local photographer, and also works in the Millinocket School System.

Frank has always enjoyed pursuing art and sharing his drawings with his children. He is an avid hiker and enjoys being able to share his love of the North Maine Woods by illustrating these Allagash Tails.